HUMANIMALS
The Book of Conscience

HUNTER MOON

ISBN 978-0-9938867-0-6

1. POETRY, General

CONTENTS

For my mother.

I'd like to give a shout out to the following people who were mentioned in my book. A special thanks to the poets Gordon Lightfoot, Neil Young, Stompin Tom Connors, Joni Mitchel, Randy Bachman, Burton Cummings, Neil Peart, Bim, Greg Keeler, Jim Cuddy, Bryan Adams, Carol Pope, Leonard Cohen, Ann Wilson and Gord Downie. Thank you for your gifts.

I'd also like to mention Spencer Sekyer, Bob Barker, and Joan Lawrence. I commend you for your caring and compassion. (All three should be cloned) I must also mention and commend Rob Ford, George Chuvalo, Wendel Clark, Justin Bieber, Constable Douglas James Larche, Constable Dave Joseph Ross, Constable Fabrice Georges Gevaudan, Nelson Mandela, Gandhi, Martin Luther King, and Bill Gates. Thank you all for supplying the much needed balance to this book. You are not Humanimals at all. Rather quite the opposite! You're the breath of fresh air. God bless you all!

I'd also like to thank Saint Francis of Assisi, my brother (and everyone's) Jesus, and God who are mentioned and who also bring a positive light to this book. And last but certainly not least, I'd like to thank my mother.

Thanks and love to all!

Hunter Moon

> *You read my book and turn the page*
> *until you see yourself*
> *And when amusement turns to rage*
> *you place it on the shelf*

INNER CORE

If your inner core is ego
and your conscience is pretended
and this book somehow offends you
you deserve to be offended

No Regrets

I killed a man once—in my youth
Who'd beat his dog up bad
Have no regrets and have the proof
Best dog I ever had

GOD BLESS HARUMBE

Harumbe the gorilla
was a kind and gentle soul
Protected a boy from danger
and that was his only goal

The people they all panicked
and thought he'd show a human trait
That of some kind of predator
That sealed him to a human fate

They gunned down poor Harumbe
They killed him in his prison home
That boy was safer with Harumbe
than with his mother who let him roam

OUIJA BOARD

When you're playing with a Ouija Board
You're playing Russian roulette
You never know what's gonna come through
You never know what you will get

You're opening up a portal
You open a darkened door
And what comes to play may decide to stay
and could ruin your life to the core

You're entertaining demons and devils
And these demons and devils aren't nice
And to keep entertained they will cause you great pain
And you may well pay a heavy price

So leave the Ouija board in the closet
Leave the Ouija board all alone
Let the devil and demons stay dormant
Never invite them into your home

DELIVERY DRIVER

He makes eight bucks an hour
delivering pizza pie
He buys his gas—there's no free pass
With out tips—tank is dry

So for all of the non—tippers
He's paying for your fare
And if you call a second time
a present may come there

He scratch to make a living
You cost him every time
So he'll add an ingredient
that you will never find

He'll think of you as you chow down
He'll drive the road you chose
He'll have less gas inside his tank
and less mess in his nose

WINDOW PANE

Fusions of illusions
dance around my mind
Reflections of deceptions
occupy my time

Things float by my window
Reflections from my brain
I'm flying my first solo
Will I be the same

Things look rather awkward
Lurching like they do
Everything looks backwards
Everything looks new

This is science fiction
A movie I am in
Tension causes friction
Stay at ease within

Everything looks solvent
Nothing has been solved
Still I sit quite content
Logic's not involved

The movie just got started
Will it ever end
Common sense departed
Will the damage mend

Gazing at the ceiling
Climbing up the wall
I've never had this feeling
I've never felt this tall

EVIL GREW

Evil grows
and evil grew
but no one knows
what evil knew

Sometimes it's black
Sometimes it's blue
It's always dark
where evil grew

It's around me
if inside you
You crack that egg
It spreads like flu

Evil grows
and evil grew
Evil you sow
Come back at you

THE ONES THAT DO

So you think that you can change the world
It's the crazy ones like you
The crazy ones who hold this thought
are the ones that usually do

Those ones who live in a world so strange
where change can change on cue
The crazy ones who do believe
are the crazy ones that do

Reverse It

Everything you do in life
to every living thing
Imagine you reverse it
What emotion does it bring

Would it bring you happiness
or would it bring you fear
Would it bring you sadness
Would it make you shed a tear

Yeah imagine you reverse it
'Cause when you die it is reversed
And you don't get to rehearse it
It's only you that you have cursed

You best treat others and our critters
with a kind and gentle touch
'Cause when you die it comes back at you
and the wave might be too much

UGLY RELIGION

Religion can get ugly
and religion can get vile
when the Prophet that you pray to
is a well known pedophile

The bride he took was only seven
when he walked her down the aisle
And she was just a child of nine
when he decided to defile

Siamese Sex

The twin brother was insistent
These twin brothers were Siamese
The left said to the right brother
Don't bring home a disease

So please put on a condom
and be quick about it please
And I will not tell mother
Just don't bring home a disease

The Charade

The Governments of Canada
dance and cater the charade
and the child abuse goes on and on
at the collective Children's Aid

Indian Act (1876)

Canada produced the Indian Act
in order to fix their so-called plight
And did so with no shame or tact
They took away the natives' rights

Their arrogance was typical
"These savages must be shown the light"
But the problem was just mythical
as the savages were all the whites!

No Warrior

My lawyer, my lawyer
He sold me down the river
He sold me down the river
for a dirty glass of water

My lawyer—no warrior
A trial would make him quiver
The thought did make him shiver
Pathetic pettifogger

GENERAL MOTORS

The mighty General Motors
came up with a plan
Abandon poor old Oshawa
and screw the little man

The little men band together
across the great divide
They won't buy G.M. trucks and cars
They're gonna find a different ride

Ones like That

I've been down to Newfoundland
and most people there are great
But with every group of people
lurks some evil—no debate

'Cause with any group of people
lurks a couple psychopaths
And the ones like that down in Newfoundland
leave a bloody aftermath

'Cause the one's like that down in Newfoundland
have the conscience of their eels
'Cause the ones like that down in Newfoundland
like to slaughter baby seals

Devil Looked Up

The devil looked up, then the devil looked down
Then he climbed up through the ground
And said: "When you least expect it—
I'm sure to be around"

"You see evils my intention
and evil is my ploy
Evil brings with it misery
The thing I most enjoy"

"So come all ye of little faith
and work into my plan
Without your faith there's no escape
and not a hope for man"

WATER

Some women walk for hours
to collect it where they can
They live in hotter climates
and have never seen a fan

We waste it 'cause we have it
Deplete it as we're fools
Some people die without it
as we fill our swimming pools

EMPATHY

It's really all about empathy
and some humans show the least
Some animals show us so much more
It's the nature of the beast

The elephants and the dolphins
have oh so, so much more
The empathy that they radiate
comes deep from in their core

When ego breeds with arrogance
the humans become beasts
Heaven help what's in their paths
when this evil is unleashed

There are some loving humans
but they're a different breed
And you can't tell the two apart
until they start to feed

MASTURBATION

Masturbation, masturbation
First time is a charm
He needs a fist of fingers
For her a finger and an arm

Masturbation cures frustration
when you're getting none
They'll be no unwanted pregnancy
for your daughter or your son

Some people do it faster
Some people do it slow
All do it well behind closed doors
But everybody knows

Masturbation's natural
It won't blind you—it never harms
If God forbid this pleasure, hid
He'd have given us shorter arms

Uninvited Odour

Your odour comes and often stuns
before you have arrived
Smells not to save—It's time to bathe
For nostrils to survive

St. Francis of Assisi

You've got to love St. Francis
if you've got any love at all
His love for all the creatures
Healing creatures big and small

The animals follow St. Francis
Walk, hop, fly, and crawl
Telepathic with St. Francis
And he hears all those who call

TEA TIME

Lady Astor and Winston Churchill
didn't get along
They gave each other quite a chill
If you don't agree—you're wrong

Lady Astor told Winston one day
that if she were his wife
She'd poison his tea—then where would he be
forever in the afterlife

Winston Churchill was quick to reply
with no need to rethink it
I don't think he lied when he replied
"If you were my wife—I'd drink it"!

SINISTER PRIME MINISTERS

From Newfoundland to Victoria
you can hear the tragic squeals
as our sinister Prime Ministers
slaughter baby seals

Conscience versus Ego

Conscience versus ego
It's the only two in play
Conscience is unconscious
when ego has it's say

Conscience versus ego
It's the only two at war
Conscience is the band aid
and ego is the sore

Conscience versus ego
is the choice you have to make
Conscience gives and gives and gives
and ego only takes

Conscience versus ego
Who's the lesser of the two
Conscience is all colours
and ego only blue

Conscience versus ego
is the choice you have to make
Ego's full of evil
as ego is the snake

Conscience versus ego
Just one choice for goodness sake
Conscience is the eagle
Let the eagle kill the snake

Conscience versus ego
And the eagle always soars
Conscience opens windows
and ego shuts the doors

Lonely House of Art

Russ lives at the lonely house
It gets lonelier by day
He once had friends that came to call
but Art chased them away

Art's the crusty old renter
He is not the house's mouse
Art the bastard rents a room
but thinks he owns the house

Art is Art—it's all about Art
Art thinks so anyway
And when Art farts he fans the air
and sends the fart your way

Art's the best at everything
At least that's what he'll say
And in Art's house you are the mouse
and Art likes it that way

Art is quite a talker
And Art will bend your ear
And Art will tell you all the things
that you don't want to hear

Art talks of his sorry life
His twenty years in jail
There's no remorse for victims
It rains—Art is the hail

Brand New Skin

Brand new skin
holds within
the wonders of the world

Brand new grin
without sin
No glass house stones to hurl

Brand new eyes
don't despise
for reasons no one knows

Brand new ears
hear the fears
but Will won't let it grow

Brand new brain
not yet trained
to plan the perfect kill

Brand new heart
Brand new part
The hatred makes heart ill

Regrets

When you're on your deathbed
counting your regrets
The deepest ones are the steepest ones
and the ones you won't forget

When you're reminiscing
and the reminisce goes amiss
Just close your eyes—try to realize
that your minutes from death's kiss

National Rifle Association (The N.R.A.)

The knife-wielding nut-bar arrives at school
He might kill two, he might kill one
The nut-bar shows up with a gun
and now he might kill every-one

The N.R.A.—they, know this
The N.R.A. don't care
The N.R.A are co-killers
It's a blame that they must share

The best way to kill a monster
You must chop off it's head
And you'll never fix this problem
until the N.R.A. is dead

The problem won't diminish
It's not going to go away
The President has to grow some balls
and squash the N.R.A.

CARTOON

The world is getting crowded
Must be running out of room
When the cowards kill the artists
just for drawing a cartoon

Je Suis Charlie

I am Charlie and I will stand
and I am not alone
And all our love will conquer hate
and all those hearts of stone

The hatred that these people breed
is so hard to conceive
The truth will hit them like freight train
when it's their turn to leave

CANADA BREEDS POETS

Canada breeds poets
and they show it and they shine
Just turn on your radio
They're playing all the time

Lightfoot, Young, and Stompin Tom
and Joni Mitchel too
Bachman, Cummings, Neil Peart and Bim
Just to name a few

Greg Keeler and Jim Cuddy
Bryan Adams, Carol Pope
All bring something to the table
Give Canadian culture hope

Did I mention Leonard Cohen
We owe nothing to the arts
Poetry is in the snow
Ann Wilson's known to melt some hearts

Each one is a great poet
As they all heard the call
It's rude to exclude Gord Downie
Maybe the greatest of them all!

How to Pray

You pray and pray and nothing happens
so you put God on a shelf
But the key to prayer is to pray for someone
other than yourself

DIVISION

All religions
cause divisions
no matter what you say

And I'll tell you this
God won't love you less
if you stay at home and pray

Drug Troll

Martin Shkreli bought the patent
for an effective cancer pill
Now unless you're filthy rich
you are screwed if you get ill

This evil, greedy, heartless troll
jacked the price times fifty-five
There's many he's put in a hole
Some can't afford to stay alive

If Karma gods pondered his fate
and came up with an answer
Logic dictates he'd have a date
with some incurable cancer

Antique Window

I bought an antique window
at the unique antique store
It wasn't for it's beauty
No there's something I want more

I bought it for the window pane
that's captured all those years
Captured all those long gone dreams
Reflected all those tears

Oh yes vibration is alive
Vibrates through out the glass
And when you die and come alive
Right through your soul may pass

WHAT IT TAKES

For all the poachers in the world
Please God do what it takes
While all of them hunt elephants
have them hunted by snakes

ALIEN SERMON

The aliens came to my home town
Once there they didn't dwell
They said: "Don't take it personal,
but we can't stand your smell"

Observed and took some mental notes
and then were on their way
"You humans here are too fucked up
This place—we cannot stay

You don't all pull together
But instead you pull apart
Your actions come straight from your head
and seldom from your heart

You walk around with masks on
Think by God you won't get busted
We'd all find it amazing
if not appalled and all disgusted

Your species as a whole's been sliced
and diced and segregated
You've made a ghost out of your Christ
It was you who separated

So as we leave we leave with you
a warning to patch holes
Your ship is sinking at God-speed
May God have mercy on your souls"

The aliens came to my home town
They didn't fair so well
They came looking for a heaven
and stumbled on our hell

Succumb

If you become the one you hate
You better hate what you become
You can't be early if you're late
and you swallow the whole sum

If you ate your plate of hate
and swallowed every crumb
It's too late to regurgitate
You surely will succumb

Nudist Camp

Those silly foolish humans
Spend their lifetime on the run
They scurry round to hide their lies
Think they're fooling everyone

They leave this earth—go through rebirth
and return to other side
That's where the lies they exercised
have nowhere now to hide

It's like going to a nudist camp
Suddenly you have no clothes
Everything's out in the open
Everything is now exposed!

Clone

Spencer Sekyer should be cloned
At least let's clone his heart
Saved a chimp from animal traffickers
and that surely is a start

Bob Barker

Bob Barker, Bob Barker
Another God should clone
He freed the elephants from their pen
and delivered them a home

The other rescued elephants
all cheered on their arrival
Bob understood this camaraderie
was Imperative to their survival

The world needs more Bob Barkers
to turn this world around
More champions for the animals
People who stand their ground

More voices for the animals
who never had a voice
More saints like Sir Bob Barker
who found them better choice

Depression

Depression's my companion
but depression's not my friend
Depression drains the life from me
and may send me round the bend

Depression goes to bed with me
and doesn't let me sleep
Depression yields no sympathy
when depression's running deep

Depression makes me shun the sun
Makes it too bright for my eyes
The sun is always going down
but I often see it rise

Depression is the darkest cloud
that gets wrapped 'round my head
Depression's like an anchor
It glues my back to my bed

FAKE NEWS

Stop reporting fake news
about the President's plight
Remember you are always wrong
and the President always right

HASH BROWNIE

Do you read my lines
once you close the blinds
and you've munched on that hash brownie

I'd rather hear "The Hip"
and the genius lip
of the man they called Gord Downie

Holocaust Down Under

The most advanced race on the planet
did not invent T.V.
Communicate to liberate
Speak through telepathy

They have a clearer vision
Something we could not see
It's not on television
so it surely could not be

They lived as one under the sun
They lived in harmony
And the white bastards that we are
We couldn't let them be

Religion ruled—Religion fooled
but fuel no empathy
The holocaust down under
The devils came by sea

The incision of their vision
was a wound you had to see
White religion was division
White's wronged rights—the right to be

NUDIST

I am a nudist—Yes I am
I take my clothes off when I can
It's not perversion—it's nothing new
I was born that way and so were you

Rape

Rape is rape—there's no debate
It can't be tolerated
And if you rape it's never too late
for you to be castrated

Rape is rape—If found guilty as charged
there should be no procrastination
Intercourse should never be forced
The penalty—castration

Men who rape and sodomise
will never be evolved
Time to cut—then cauterize
and then the problem's solved!

THE MAN WHO WALKS AMONG THE STARS

The Man Who Walks Among The Stars
is up there looking down
He muses 'bout the natives plight
Has rite to wear a frown

Started discussion while down on earth
Now we must keep it going
We gotta shrink the way we think
before they can start growing

My Lawyer

I didn't trust my lawyer
as far as I could throw him
And if you seem to disagree
you surely do not know him

TWITTER AWAY

Look down when you twitter
Look up when you fall
Life is just a flicker
and you're missing it all

You're missing reflection
Alone in your own head
A certain direction
we all need to be led

Time spent with your conscience
leads your head to your heart
They have to get closer
Not get farther apart

You've missed mother nature
The birds flying by
The wonder of nature
on land and in sky

You're missing the sunset
The kite in the air
The screen radiates
and you're caught in the glare

BILL COSBY

They slapped the cuffs on Cosby
and hauled him off to jail
The day of reckoning for the rapist
The judge refused him bail

America's favorite father
was a monster in disguise
The monster has been caught and caged
And for Cosby—no reprise

He raped some sixty women
There could be many more
Bill Cosby is a monster
Bill Cosby is a whore

And now the monster rots in jail
For Bill there's no recourse
And what reaffirms he's a monster
He's shown us no remorse

Sixty times

You'd have to clone the bastard sixty times
to serve time for all his sixty crimes
Sixty times the gavel falls
Sixty times build four more walls

Falcon Girl

William Melchert-Dinkel
In his house he'd hide
Trolling on the Internet
to persuade suicide

Pretending he was Falcon Girl
A man of forty-six
He'd talk girls through their suicide
That's how Dinkel got his kicks

ALL FALL DOWN

We all get up—We all fall down
but some throw others to the ground
I just don't like those types around
It's best to lose them I have found

SIRUS

My name is Sirus
I am a virus
And that is what I am

I'll infect you
And right on cue
If you stick to the plan

I lurk inside
the skin you ride
and then I enter you

I'll wear you down
I'll stretch the ground
Then shrink you through and through

You'll make a wish
in petri dish
And that's a dime you blew

If I get inside
I got a ride
until I bury you

EVIL WEED

The old man he did lecture them
He said stay off the pot
If you smoke that evil weed
your brain will surely rot

He said they'd wile away their lives
by writing dreamy poems
First sleeping on their best friends couch
Then breaking in their homes

REVENGE

A lesson for those who seek revenge
that you should not forget
If your means to an end is to avenge
You probably will regret

SHUTTLE DRIVER

I'm a shuttle driver
I shuttle folks around
I shuttle here and I shuttle there
and I shuttle all over town

I'm a real observer
Converse and listen real hard
I separate the genuine people
from the ones so full of lard

I like genuine people
You can almost feel their heart
They're funny and warm and they don't swarm
From the others—they're miles apart

The others are a one way ticket
To the centre of their dim light
Self—obsessed, almost possessed
and oh so wrapped up tight

Drinking from a Puddle

Drinking from a puddle in a parking lot
That's what's left for geese
All the green space has been bought
The geese have lost their lease

Hired Gun

In the shell of the hell of divorce
It gets uglier the more that you make
It ain't about what they can get
It's more about what they can take

I'm not talking about your ex-partner
from the marriage you want to expire
I'm talking about the real winners
That's the lawyers you both had to hire

Final Jab

He could have been this
He might have been that
The cowards tongues do roam
As they whisper at his visitation
inside the funeral home

LIAR LIAR

I heard something said about him
while walking down the street
It must be true—It must be true
A lie like that you would not repeat

Until We Meet Again

I think I knew you long ago
when we lived back on earth
It's been two hundred years or so
since I went through that birth

I lived down there one hundred years
Sometimes it felt much more
I did my time and lost my fears
and faced my inner core

We all were sent upon that trip
to test our free will flow
Our actions were observed up here
although we didn't know

Our secrets are not secrets
There are no secrets here
When you arrive you come alive
All secrets reappear

A secret's not a secret
when everyone's aware
And when you do arrive up here
we all know what you did down there

BRUCE MCARTHER

Bruce McArther, what a monster
The victim list does grow
Eight victims found—how many more?
We'll probably never know

DEVIL'S MEAL

A plate of Veal—The devil's meal
with what the calves go through
And if you eat a plate of Veal
then you the devil too

Their entire life—a few short months
in utter hopelessness
Force fed, crated—Alone in dark
Pure hell—this human mess

MICROSCOPE

They legalized Marijuana
and it's getting hard to cope
The cops got all the tokers
under giant microscope

You can't toke here—You can't smoke there
Before they didn't care
They see red eyes—surprise—you're high
The cops are everywhere

LATE NIGHT LEAK

The night is cold
It doesn't matter
I must relieve
my so full bladder

Out to the outhouse
I must be bold
Until the morning
I cannot hold

A good nights sleep
I cannot seek
until I take
this mighty leak

A fleeting moment
I quickly think
Should I relieve
myself in sink

The consequences
If I get caught
They'll tie my dick
into a knot

Your Children

Your children are your everything
You've loved them since they're small
If you give them everything
you don't help them at all

Very Stable Genius

Claims he's a very stable genius
and richer than he is
Claims he has a larger penis
than what is really his

Well I don't care about his fare
and what Trump has to say
I know a very stable genius
would terminate the N.R.A.

Tragedy

I'm sorry 'bout your tragedy
as you can surely see
But I must say quite truthfully
I'm glad it wasn't me

THE DROOLER

The drooler Jaylon Kerley
Is quite the little shit
Selling slices of pizza
which he covered with his spit

He posted it on Instagram
His second bad decision
He was arrested and now he faces
four long years in prison

WITHER

Through the rage that you engage
and oh I know it well
You may just wither as you age
but only time will tell

If you wither you may slither
like the snake you are
Shed your skin and then begin
to hunt for your lost star

Lost star in a sky—full bright
Been swallowed by the moon
And in its turn the sun will burn
the moon—a burst balloon

And on and on, and on and on
And everything's a chain
Cycles run in circles
Concept hard to explain

And it always goes full circle
And it always comes around
And it always gains momentum
but it never makes a sound

So it blindsides you times eighty
Another Karma kind of thing
And what the wind brings to the table
Are the things you used to bring

PISTOL WHIPPED

The hunters show up with their dogs
What they kill the dogs will find
They have their fun and then they run
and leave their dogs behind

The dogs—they die a horrible death
They starve or they are eaten
These hunters should be rounded up
and pistol whipped and beaten

HITLER'S BABYSITTER

If I was Hitler's babysitter
and could go back in time
I'd drowned him in the bathtub
and do time for my crime

Oh who could kill a baby
Oh no never me
But to kill a baby monster
A better place the world would be!

Evil Beach in Argentina

There's a beach in Argentina
where pure evil can be found
Where they caught a baby dolphin
and passed him all around

So they all could take their selfies
they caused the baby dolphin's death
The pure evil of some people
It makes you lose your breath

Once they got their pictures
they placed the dolphin on the ground
He should have been saved by a tidal wave
and these bastards would have drowned

Fire Pit

If I should go before my time
and suddenly expire
Meet me by my fire pit
and light me one more fire

I'll be a ghost but I will host
The fire will be grand
I'll dance in flames—burn my remains
before I leave this land

Wrong Stuff

There comes a time
Your body fails and says enough's enough
If you inhale, inject, ingest
any of the wrong stuff

It will catch up
Tortoise and Hare—and you are running late
This is a race that you won't win
It all accumulates

REFLECTION

Look into the mirror my friend
and look hard if you can
Are you looking at a boy
or looking at a man

Which is the reflection
Tell me if you can
Have you stayed a boy or died
and morphed into a man

When you lose your innocence
There goes the whole plan
The dead inside the boy
becomes the led inside the man

ROB FORD

Rob Ford admitted his faults
Not an easy thing to do
And a task that's even harder
He admitted them all to you

Good Lord—open up the vaults
Let the great unwashed pass through
Well hidden in their closets
there's a skeleton or two

Rob Ford—where the buck halted
Didn't pass the buck on cue
Was a caring politician
Heard the little guy's point of view

Good Lord—Give the man a break
He served well when he served you
He got clean and he got sober
The peoples Mayor through and through

SONS OF TRUMP

The sons of Trump—they like to hunt
Big Game—which isn't ample
And if they hunt an elephant
I hope the Trumps get trampled

Rebecca Francis

Is Rebecca Francis a psychopath
She smiles in photo with dead Giraffe
In photo Rebecca looks so thrilled
with dead Giraffe that she just killed

Did something bad happen in her youth
to Rebecca Francis—that photo's proof
Something in her just ain't right
Thrilled to kill and then delight

Heal

Putting child killers in healing centers
It takes away your breath
The only way to heal these folks
is to put them all to death

To do that deed—can't let them breed
You surely cannot fix 'em
There's only one solution then
I guess you have to nix 'em

LOAD

My brother lives up the river
and I'm pissed as you can see
'Cause when he pees in the river
he pees all over me

I'm gonna leap frog up the river
Then I'll eat enough to explode
Gonna wade into that river
Drop a log jam of a load

Let that load float down the river
There's no need to draw a map
It will find its way to my brother's bay
He can then deal with my crap

BALD SPOT

The frontal bald spot meets the rear
and your hairline erases
The hairs not gone—so have no fear
It's moved to other places

It's in your ears—it's up your nose
and the other orifices
You pluck it out and back it grows
A cruel metamorphosis

Governments

The arrogance of Governments
So many in a fog
It's not so much the things they say
It's the way that they play God

The plastic in the ocean
The smog that clogs the air
Self serving—shelf deserving
Most are carnivores—beware!

First humans ran the governments
It then got turned around
Now everybody scurries
Buries nuts well underground

Some governments never relent
It's take and take and take
But sympathy don't pay the rent
When broke—easy to break

LESSER MINDS

To the educated people
who think lesser minds need feeding
While you dosed off at the lecture
I was wide awake and reading

SNOW-SQUALLS

Upstairs neighbor—Cocaine dealer
Up and down the stairs all night
Here them coming—here them going
Snow-squalls blowing till daylight

Creepy crawlers, Midnight brawlers,
Darkness dwellers rarely sleep
The moon rises—no surprises
Cocaine brains begin to creep

BIRDS

Water, land, and air
Birds go everywhere
Fly without a care
until it's hunting season

Birds fly high and scared
when the sky is shared
with lead that tends to tear
and sent for just that reason

MENNONITE TOWN

The Mennonites
might have it right
as they move from chore to chore

In a Mennonite town
when the sun goes down
you needn't lock your door

In a Mennonite town
when the sun goes down
you'll never have to run

The Mennonites
have no will to fight
Have no need to point a gun

Pigs

The humans gather up the pigs
and send them off to slaughter
The mother pig is terrified
for both her son and daughter

The humans they don't really care
They have a taste for bacon
They don't believe the pigs' fear's real
but boy are they mistaken

The humans once again believe
that they have all the answers
The fear instilled returns to kill
Returns as random cancer

Teenage Perspective

The twenty year old was quite impressed
Squashed his genetic fears
Was amazed how much his old man had learned
in only three short years

TARNISHED SWASTIKA

The Hindus and the Buddhists
want their swastika back
It was stolen by the Nazis
and is all tarnished and black

Once a sign of good fortune
but the Nazis changed all that
It is now a sign of evil
and there is no turning back

THE BETTERTHANS

I went to breakfast with the Betterthans
Their meal was better than mine
Their vacations were better
The weather was better
and they had a better time

I went to lunch with the Betterthans
They had a better time than I
Chose a better soup
Wore a better suit
and he had a better tie

I missed my dinner with the Betterthans
And I didn't miss it at all
Didn't miss the slaps
Didn't miss the crap
Didn't miss the utter gall

BEAR WALKER

I'm a Bear walker my friend
and I can walk through walls
And you won't even know I'm there
The times I come to call

I'm a Bear walker my friend
and what I see is all
What soon becomes my window
will always be your wall

Trap the Trapper

I'd like to set off the trapper's traps
Put his fingers in there as he sleeps or he naps
When the spring is sprung the trapper reels
and now the sick bastard knows just how it feels

BIEBER FEVER

My daughter's got the Bieber fever
I don't know what to do
This shouldn't be a problem
but my daughter's forty-two

Justin is her Beaver Cleaver
She sings his songs on cue
This wouldn't be a problem
if she wasn't forty-two

She's a real conniver
Drunken driver of the screw
She's the cougar of the litter
and I don't know what to do

'Cause the fever will not leave her
and she's got a bluish hue
She could have been his babysitter
'cause my daughter's forty-two

MAN IN BLACK (MIB)

The beast came in my room one night
A darkened figure—shed no light
Standing over, staring down
Black Stetson, or maybe brown

I was a child of four or five
The figure's cold, but still alive
I felt his icy frostbit stare
I'm haunted by that evil glare

I ran right by the living dead
and headed to my parents bed
I woke them up and spoke of it
The monster from the devil's pit

My parents led me to my room
Turned on the light, dispersed the gloom
The beast was gone—not seen again
His stare's embedded in my brain

It had black coat, it was no dream
and evil seeped from every seam
I haven't seen it since that night
But even now it sends a fright

I was a child of four or five
The figure's old but still alive
Evil lurks on earth to dwell
I've met the one who holds its spell

OVAL OFFICE

You can't buy the Oval office
but it appears it is for rent
But the lease expires in four years
for an awful President

ALIEN INTERVENTION

We need Alien intervention
A species most malevolent
To put the human race back in its place
A clear mirror of our intent

I'm not talking everybody
Let the aliens take out the crap
Show them fear like they spread down here
Wake their conscience from its nap

A cleansing of our planet
A flushing of bad souls
Let the alien detect human sin
then dispatch them to black holes

Yeah we need an alien species
that's selectively malevolent
Who can sort through all the humans
Remove all with bad intent

Wouldn't the world be beautiful
It would be a brand new birth
The hell in that we live right now
would become heaven on this earth

COPENHAGEN ZOO

Bengt Holst is the director
of the Copenhagen zoo
He's more like a dictator
and the animals—his muse

He slaughtered little Marius
after breakfast of rye bread
An eighteen—month baby giraffe
He shot him in the head

Then Bengt Holst killed once again
A family of four lions
Young cubs and parents had no chance
once Holst decides they're dying

Please someone stop this evil man
so decent folk can smile
Wrap him up in rye bread
and feed him to the crocodile

Frightened Fools

There wasn't one man in that Taliban clan
Just a bunch of frightened fools
And what were they so frightened of?
A little girl that went to school

Relatives

Some relatives aren't relative
when they're outta sight
Avoid the ones that are always wrong
and think they're always right

The one's with all the answers
who really aren't that bright
I'd rather run away from them
than stick around and fight

SECRETS CAN'T ESCAPE

Your secrets can't escape it
There is no where to hide
All of us are making movies
which are watched on other side

Over here you cover up those scenes
Over there—they're all exposed
Over there you remove layers
And not ashamed to shed those clothes

LIFER

He struts around like a proud peacock
thinking he's the man
Spent twenty years in a prison cell
burning tattoos on his hands

Hordes his clothes—'cause what he knows
is regulation gear
He wore, he walked, he ate, he talked
what was bellowed in his ear

He still steals lighters at the local store
Feels it's his redemptious right
There is no courage in this core
A bark without a bite

If you see him in the neighbourhood
he'll tell you he's the man
He is, he was, and always will be
the man without a plan

THE ONES I'VE MET (BIGOTS)

The ones I've met
get in my face
With no regret
displace my race

The ones I've met
think they're the ones
The safest bet
The chosen sons

The ones I've met
fall fast—retard
No safety net
and concrete's hard

The one's I've met
fall hard like rain
And once they're wet
always leave stain

PIRANHA SNACKS

He swam Piranha infested waters
to reach his destiny
He still has hands and legs to stand
but now sits down to pee

GEORGE CHUVALO

George Chuvalo—one tough boxer
who's had a tougher life
Sent Ali to the hospital
then went dancing with his wife

His endurance and his inner strength
are something to behold
When God made George Chuvalo
he threw away the mold

Bring the Day

Probably not or no
That's the way they go
All the negative people
ride the negative flow

Not going to happen—no way
That's what they all say
To achieve you must believe
that you can bring the day

Animal Suit

Put a human soul in an animal suit
and see how it survives
Sealed in fur, claws, and mute
No progress—no surprise

Thoughts capacitate—can't communicate
Makes it hard to build a machine
Claws dictate—cannot create
Impossible package for a dream

Put an animal soul housed in human form
A better world starts to thrive
Reversed roles—altered from the norm
and the animal stays alive

SMOKE SCREEN

They wait outside the Vatican
waiting for Holy smoke
They wait for white smoke signal
that verifies a new Pope

The Cardinals then collect the smoke
and capture it in vials
And save it for the smoke screen
that hides their pedophiles

Brother to All

Got to live in this old world
where they crucified our brother
And in two-thousand plus years
God has never sent another

And the evil grows and grows
and it really starts to smother
But to stay out of its throes
we must talk more to our brother

Monsters of South Korea

The Dog farms of South Korea
are seventeen thousand strong
They slaughter two and a half million dogs a year
Hell—Yeah something is wrong

The Monsters of South Korea
May God strike them down from above
To abuse, terrify, then slaughter
a being that's so full of love

Oh God please fix South Korea
and give their dogs a better fate
than to be abused, beaten, then eaten
Served up on a damned dinner plate

BORN OR BRED

The heart don't work
All reactions from the head
Are they born
or are they bred

Psychopath with heart
forged out of lead
Were you born
or were you bred

Nothing Worse

In life—there must be nothing worse
than to place your child into the earth
The one you've nurtured since their birth
In life—there's nothing that is worse

SMITTEN

Fred was smitten with a real sex kitten
but the lady was a whore
So Fred got laid but since has paid
as he wound up with a sore

Fred got chills—the doctor gave him pills
and the sore it went away
Now his hand does roam when he's all alone
He's still smitten to this day

COCAINE

Cocaine
It's in his brain
He's crouched and staring
in the pouring rain

Paranoid
Delusion fills the void
Confusions his illusion
as realities destroyed

Too much
He's out of touch
What was his cane
has become his crutch

Mr. President

The forty-sixth will be the one
to rearrange what has been done
The forty-sixth will be the first
to clean the mess up of the worst

Red Tears

A person of conscience would starve
before they'd slaughter a baby seal
Look into theirs and their mothers eyes
The tears that they shed are so real

WICKED WORLD

The world is so much darker
in its collective attitude
It's now your right to be impolite
and quite righteous to be rude

How do you do? Hell no—screw you!
It's all for one and none for all
Bleed on the sidewalk until you're blue
We're here to help but please don't call

Reptilians

Some lawyers are like reptiles
Gotta hit them with a rake
 Some are soft shell turtles
and others rattlesnakes

Collect all anti-venom
Ten vials of all they make
Some lawyers are quite harmless
But some venomous snakes

PATHETIC LITTLE MAN

Stephane Gendron is the mayor
of Huntingdon, Quebec
This pathetic little man
is more a human wreck

He admits to killing kitty cats
with his pick-up truck
I pray and pray to see the day
when he runs out of luck

While driving in his pick-up truck
A foggy night with rain
An unseen rail-road crossing
sees this bastard crushed by train

Soul-less

Message to Paul Bernardo
Stay well down in your hole
Surviving victims relive hell
each time you seek parole

If you had any kind of conscience
or any kind of soul
You'd leave these shattered folk alone
and never seek parole

You're never gonna get it
You've got no chance in hell
So shut your mouth except your fate
Stay in your crate—your cell

IMPEACHED

Ethics and Integrity
are qualities you cannot teach
And a President with neither
You surely must impeach

President Trump has been impeached
but his trial was all for naught
The Republicans knew he was guilty
but didn't want him to get caught

The Republicans wanted no witnesses
Wanted them to all shut up
With no witnesses there's no trial
Just a giant cover-up

When the Republicans were successful
and the witnesses had no say
That's the cue for America to unite as one
and kick Trump out on election day

To re-elect this President
would be a dangerous thing
A President without reproach
ain't a President—it's a King

Mill Pond Scum

The punks come slither to Mill Pond
in search of wood and stone
to decorate and desecrate
as if it were their own

They kill the view with black and blue
Leave your spray paint at home
Get out of here and take your beer
Leave well enough alone

Awful Poet

Just who is this awful poet
Sarcastic bastard full of hate
A champion fart and fine dart thrower
Thinks he's better to berate

In real life he's far from perfect
Then who is—we're on the wheel
treading faster from disaster
All here to even karma deal

So be careful on this journey
and I will try to do the same
Treat the good folk like they're good folk
and all the others—lay the blame

THE WHEEL

I throw the dirt
but don't be hurt
It's not all that you see

I have my faults
and they don't halt
so throw some dirt on me

We're here to heal
That's why we're here
That's why we're on the wheel

We spin around
First up then down
We all need sympathy

TAR

We battered up the brownies
Eight grams of blackened tar
We gobbled down—then took a hike
but didn't get too far

We made it to the river
then lay upon the ground
And we stayed there for quite awhile
Our private lost and found

Thorn and Thistle

Thorn, Thistle, beasts of prey
Human thought brought them to play
Insects swarm the earth and breed
Brought by evil thoughts and greed

CARCASS

To be a man in Pakistan
you must be prepared to slaughter
To uphold family honour
you may kill your wife or daughter

The killing restores their honour
in a very twisted culture
The body becomes a carcass
and the spectators the vultures

SHERIFF CECIL PRICE

Long ago in Mississippi
lived Sheriff Cecil Price
Cecil was a bad guy
Yeah Cecil wasn't nice

He handed three Civil Rights workers
over to the K.K.K.
They killed the three—no sympathy
Price was the one who paved the way

RETALIATE

We kill the earth
Earth is in pain
Retaliates
Sends hurricane

She bring the fire
before the rain
To burn the straws
and cellophane

The straws alone
clog up her drain
She'll wash away
the human stain

Extinct

The big game hunter/slash/asshole's dead
Now he rests in mausoleum
He's surrounded by his trophy heads
if the public wants to see 'em

The lion head, the rhino head
and every kind of fur
You can look at them and pat them
but you'll never hear them purr

You see the assholes went and killed them
and not one of them did think
of repercussions of their actions
and soon all will be extinct

SNAKE CHARMER

The cops—they all surround the house
and you gotta know who sent 'em
'Cause the one who brings the snake
is the one who brings the venom

And the venom you can't shake
You can feel it in your tendons
It may be more than you can take
and if you break who's left to bend 'em

FORTY DAYS

Forty days is all you need
Forty days will plant the seed
Forty days will turn you pale
if you spend forty days in jail

Forty days and forty nights
in a dim but constant light
It's dimmest in the dead of night
It's all left turns and never right

Days are nights and nights are day
It's always going to be that way
With no sleep they blend into one
and in a cage—no where to run

THREE BRAVE MEN

The Mounties buried three brave men
Brave men who gave their lives
The only braver in Moncton
were the three brave Mounties wives

Constables Larche, Ross, and Gevaudan
are heroes one and all
And when our lives were all at risk
all three answered the call

Three stetson wearing angels
stepped up when danger came
All three shot dead in cold blood
by a bastard I won't name

Pecker's Toward Air

The rules for males when skinny dipping
Pecker's up and toward air
You never know what's lurking
May be leering from down there

A Muskie or a Snapping Turtle
could cause you great despair
One quick crunch—your pecker's lunch
So keep it pointed towards air

I find when I go skinny dipping
I spin and I rotate
That way the prey's not focused
and this saves my pecker from that fate!

Westboro Baptist Church

Somewhere down in Kansas
resides the Westboro Baptist Church
where they love to spew their hatred
from well up on their perch

They claim that God hates sinners
and so-called sinners go to hell
These pathetic small-brained people
are mentally not well

This clan—that's so judgemental
and so quick with evil eye
will get more than what they bargained for
the blessed day they die

SOME KIND OF SIN

No gays allowed in the house of God
The Calvary Baptist church forbade 'em
Tim Wagner give your head a shake
and realize God's the one that made 'em

Wagner's the Deacon chairman
of the Calvary Baptist church
We need inclusion not exclusion
So you know where to shove your perch

The Baptists wait at Heaven's gate
and no one let's them in
A religion fueled by so much hate
is some kind of a sin

MOTHMAN

December sixth in Eighty-nine
The biggest loser—Marc Lepine
He took his life after his crime
The biggest coward of all time

The girls he killed were butterflies
The moth he was—I do despise
I wish that he had found the flame
before he became Quebec's shame

DR. DOODNAUGHT

Dr. George Doodnaught
 is quite easy to abhor
He's not much of a doctor
Quite the slimy little whore

Dr. George Doodnaught
is really quite pathetic
Sexually abused his patients
once they're under anaesthetic

ALZHEIMER'S

The Alzheimer's got hold of him
Connections did get burned
In time he has forgotten
more than he had ever learned

Life becomes illusion
Television twilight zone
And to add to the confusion
emptiness has found a home

Hell for family—they go through it
All its waters are unknown
And the loved one never knew it
Sometimes hell to be full grown

Hang 'Em High

Judge John Wood was no good
so someone shot him down
Saved some souls he would have froze
Judge John Wood was a clown

With alibi—still hung 'em high
That was Judge John Woods' way
Judge Woods' death was a fresh breath
and John Woods' finest day

CONSCIENCE OF A DREAM

The animals that suffer
A cruel life from what I've seen
Please tell me life is not real
We're just the conscience of a dream

The conscience of a dream
Conscience or lack there of
As God studies our thought patterns
and takes notes from above

EVIL BREED

You see the mug shot—See the stare
and you can tell there's nothing there
No compassion—No remorse
The crimes for some—Par for the course

Out there among us—Evil breed
Born evil from evil seed
Evil hides and evil smirks
and in your garden evil lurks

FINANCIAL ADVISOR

I'm your financial adviser
You should listen to what I say
If you don't heed my advice
your fortune may slip away

If you win the Lotto jackpot
I'd advise you build a vault
and if your friends turn into leaches
you should buy a bag of salt

If your giving, they'll start taking
They'll want more and more and more
As your bank account is dwindling
you've become a money store

One

One race—different shades
One class—different grades
One choice—seek the truth
One voice—regain youth

One sky—many storms
One rose—many thorns
One path—others worn
One lie—others born

One web—many strands
One grip—many hands
One time—feel the need
One crime—fueled by greed

One clock—time ticks on
One note—not a song
One day—will we feel
One life—make it real

Karma

Those who hurt our animals
don't know the Karma wheel
For every pain that they inflict
Jesus is sure to feel

All the pains recorded
It never ever peels
And when your sent back home my fiend
The pain you're sure to feel

And for every second
that seemed to be a year
You will fear the pain my fiend
and you will feel the fear

That's the laws of nature
and that's what you should know
You always keep and always reap
the harvest that you sow

And so for every second
you get a year of fear
And you will feel the pain my fiend
as Jesus sheds a tear

Never Intertwined

Your conscience and your ego
are never intertwined
Your conscience is a flower
Your ego just a vine

Conscience gives you beauty
Your ego makes you blind
The flower loses power
when it's strangled by the vine

THE SEVENTH DIRECTION

The seventh direction
is the one with infection
that the people have to clear

The first insight
is their only rite
Holds the answer to the sphere

The final thought
is the one that's caught
It's the sum of all its parts

The final light
will heed all insight
Pave a path back to their heart

The seventh direction
is an outward direction
Is the one that's without sin

Radiates past Mars
seeking distant stars
And it starts from deep within

TIME WITH JESUS

I spent some time with Jesus
It was just before my birth
It was a lovely moment
He told me of my worth

If you think I think I'm special
you just haven't got a clue
'Cause just before your very birth
you spent time with Jesus too

You surely don't remember
That is part of the plan
But keep him closer to your heart
'cause Jesus is the man

He's not in high—tech gadgets
but he is all around
You may be aware—if you dare
to put those gadgets down

He's not in your computer
but he's all over town
He's never seen on the big screen
but Jesus gets around

He's living all around us
He lives in your third world
He suffers with the ones who do
Turns a shell into a pearl

Passing Wind

Passing wind, passing wind
Let it out—don't keep it in
Fan the blanket—it ain't no sin
Once it's out you can't rescind

Don't bottle it—that nauseous gas
Just let it out—just let it pass
But please don't point that nauseous ass
If you're a lad—you'll lose your lass

Open window—let in air
Light a match—that's if you dare
Post a sign—that's if you care
Passing wind so just beware

THE CARDS YOU PLAY

Dogs and cats are full of love
and sent to us from God above
And yes you will incur regrets
if you abuse God's beloved pets

Placed in your hands their fate you hold
How you treat them comes back ten-fold
If you abuse and terrify
It all comes back the day you die

So read this poem and roll your eyes
Remember shit attracts the flies
Karma's fast and Karma's real
The cards you play will seal your deal

ABORIGINAL

The primitive and "civilized"
couldn't reach a compromise
So the primitive were forced to live
in the white man's world of lies

The primitive were all baptised
into the white man's world of lies
And you gotta know—through God's own eyes
Who really were the civilized

DR. REKHI

Dr. Rekhi is the vet from hell
An animal lover he ain't
If someone beat him half to death
My God they'd be a saint

He abused the animals in his care
This monster is quite ruthless
Just him and me—five minutes alone
This bastard would be toothless

THE LOAN ARRANGER

I trust the loan arranger
when I need some cash
I'll grab some beer and season cheer
There's a party near to crash

I went and crashed that party
I won't tell the whole tale
but now the loan arranger
must bail me out of jail

I trust the loan arranger
to go into his stash
That way when I get out on bail
Won't have to dine and dash

POET WITH CREDIT

I'm a starving Poet
but I got credit all over town
I can grab a slice of pizza
and I put nothing down

Want to make it as a Poet
Yeah wouldn't that be nice
Walk into that pizza shop
and pay cash for that slice

CELEBRITY

If I was a celebrity
Would I really want to be?
Camera crews all over me
Watch myself on T.M.Z.

Have to turn off my T.V.
Quite life—serenity
All of that is history
 Private life will never be

I don't think that is for me
Everything for all to see
Prying eyes don't cover me
Can't reverse celebrity

BROKEN CHAIN

The second victim turned
to the one first burned
and said: Why didn't you tell
If you had told before you were old
I wouldn't have gone through hell
And then the third
who'd heard every word
To the second he did turn
If you had told before you were old
I'd have escaped my turn
And then the fourth turned to him
and the fifth did begin
and the broken chain goes on
And the silence kills
with intense chills
from a scar that's never gone
Well the sixth was bold
and the sixth he told
and the monster rots in jail
'Cause the sixth was brave
Not a slave to grave
in the monsters sordid tale

Night Visit

I like to visit
Mill pond at night
I see half of the garbage
Darkness dulls my sight

I see all of the garbage
in the bright day light
That's why I visit
Mill pond at night

Biggest Coward Ever

The students in Parkland, Florida
couldn't find a place to hide
As the biggest coward ever
Deputy Peterson hid outside

The nut-bar loser Nikolas Cruz
 shot them one by one
And Scot Peterson, a deputy
was at the school and had a gun

That twisted loser Nikolas Cruz
killed the kids he overpowered
and all the while armed deputy
Scot Peterson hid and cowered

Beer for Santa

We left Santa two ice cold beers
He swallowed every drop
I figured out in later years
my father disliked milk and pop

THE ASSASSIN

The assassin dies
and meets his past prey
Who take pleasure informing him
that he cannot stay

They're now free of this earth
but the assassin returns
And now he's the victim
'cause now it's his turn

PLASTIC DISASTER

Five trillion pieces of plastic
in our oceans and seas
Killing all the ocean life
Already brought it to its knees

Plastic bottles, plastic bags
There's plastic everywhere
There's plastic straws up turtles' snouts
'cause all the assholes just don't care

The polluters are the assholes
Human garbage—lazy pricks!
Lets drown them in the ocean
and then half the problem's fixed

SWALLOWED

The seal hunters got swallowed
by the unforgiving sea
And the sinking of their vessel
brought no tears to taint my tea

And the bastards died a horrible death
but I have no sympathy
It's a little thing called Karma
Could it be their destiny?

GODLESS GOVERNMENT

The Islamic Government of Iran
should be shot, pissed on and flogged
Then string them up and lynch them all
for how they treat their dogs

IVORY

It's time to wake up Asia
'Cause it's a damned disgrace
Their ridiculous quest for ivory
another Rhino lost its face

And of their quest for ivory
It doesn't do a thing
Won't make it grow or make it hard
 It won't help their ding-a-ling

Help Wanted (Heartless)

We're seeking the coldest of cold people
No apathy required
In fact it'd be a detriment
for the people that we hire

We're looking for the heartless
Not for the feign of heart
You cannot care—need an icy stare
to tear the puppies world apart

You'll be working in a test lab
and some chemicals do burn
To make make-up safe, many puppies shaved
and every puppy gets its turn

You cannot flinch when they cry and whimper
Oh how fast these puppies age
At the end of day—no love or play
Just isolation in cold, hard cage

That's the norm for the labs in Canada
For the country that boasts it's kind
Truth be told Canada can be evil and cold
to let a tragedy like this unwind

State Rape

Raped by the state
before he was eight
Cried out for help
but help showed up late

Turned into a man
who'd been drained since his birth
Who had no empathy
for a soul here on earth

Society made him
He always claimed
There's some truth to that
Charles Manson was his name

Hunters

Hunters kill the mother
and hunters kill the calves
Hunting is the pleasure
shared by psychopaths

Lets go out and buy some land
that provides little cover
We'll take all of the hunters there
and let them hunt each other

Free Will Flow

Heaven on earth was long ago
Before we had free will
When free will flow—yes became no
Conceived, then birth—evil

Ego, greed—had need to feed
It all went out of wack
The soul less seed—a different breed
What we had is what they lack

Ego conceived—conscience relieved
The cyclone spins around
And lots were lost but not retrieved
'cause nothing has been found

A different world on planet Earth
Now caught in evil spell
We conceived and then gave birth
to this world we've christened "Hell"

REINCARNATION

Before you blame your loss on God
and put him on the shelf
He didn't choose this life for you
You chose it for yourself

You drew the chart—now play your part
for advancement of your soul
The chart you drew will expand you
and help fill in the hole

It's all about eternal life
This life is just a blink
We're all just actors in this play
All actors on the brink

You chose all of the valleys
You chose all of the peaks
You chose all of the ups and downs
What harvest you would reap

It's called Reincarnation
We're all just on the wheel
And if you want off of this ride
you've got to learn to feel

You've got to learn compassion
A lot more empathy
You've got to reign in your free will
You've got to learn to see

LEPROSY

On Valentines day we'll buy a rose
Somewhere a child just lost their nose
They've lost their fingers and their toes
all to the poor mans plague

Leprosy could have been cured
had the Western world not been obscured
with shallowness and focus blurred
and a conscience that's so vague

GAMBLERS

If you're ample and gamble
You gamble for greed
If you scramble to gamble
You gamble to feed

The greed in a gambler
It starts with a seed
The smaller your bundle
The bigger the need

The grip of the gamble
An ace high to lead
You pull on the handle
The greed starts to breed

DADDY'S CADDY

Self-made billionaire
Oh please—that's just a joke
Daddy Fred lit the bonfire
and Donald just blew smoke

Trump claims to be a Genius
The consummate businessman
But Donald would be penniless
without the help of his old man

The Trump dynasty was sinking
so Donald called up daddy
And once again Fred bailed him out
Fred was the player—Donald the caddy

Place Called Hell

Murder, rape, decapitate
and everything in between
There's only one animal culpable
and that's the human being

We claim to be superior
than all life forms where we dwell
But God knows better—that's why we're promised
a little place called Hell!

ABDUCTION

The bush plane circled, then it lands
Took native children by the hand
From their parents, they're separated
The native children segregated

Separated by many miles
Hand delivered to pedophiles
Their parents never had a say
as all the children became prey

It might be Canada's greatest shame
The white race, once again to blame
What makes this outrage more insane
It started long before the plane

INCEL REBELLION

Alek Minassian muttered
"I'm afraid of girls"
Had a solution to his problem
in his sordid, twisted world

Another Incel rebellion
This helped form his plan
If he couldn't get a girl
He surmised—nobody can

He idolized another loser
who once had done the same
I won't glorify that loser
by mentioning his name

Minassian killed ten people
and injured fifteen more
Acted out his plan in a rental van
A nut bar evil to the core

Two kilometers of carnage
He did not discriminate
He hit anyone and everyone
Can't understand his hate

Now my hometown is in tatters
but Toronto will stand tall
And we'll all heal 'cause it matters
that we stand up after fall

MANDELA'S LEAGUE

Just who is in Mandela's league
Only just a few
Gandi, Martin Luther King
Are they the only two

Not many more could hold the door
I say with no debate
There is another in this league
His name—Mr. Bill Gates

HOLY GRAIL

When God gave us free will
It's like we're under spell
We took the world he gave us
and turned it into hell

The animals—our children
We started to devour
Fore sake all that was sacred
It was not our finest hour

Free will led to ill will
That's the pill we had to swallow
The warmth became a chill
and the whole became all hollow

And now the evil's rampant
as devices replace God
And the feel replaces real
The Holy Grail's now the iPod

Gold Digger

Gold digger look
Gold digger see
Gold digger want no part of me

Sell some books
and we shall see
Gold digger—she all over me

Carnivore

He loves his meat
He's a meat whore
Beware the mighty carnivore

He doesn't hiss
He doesn't roar
He's man and he's a carnivore

He'll eat your feet
Then want some more
Hey bear—beware the carnivore

BEAST CALLED GREED

I'm on the plains of Africa
and I am on the hunt
I'm looking for her litter
Especially the runt

I'm hunting down a beast called greed
As evil as they come
Has tentacles called poachers
at the wrong end of a gun

Gonna get a helicopter
Mount a couple machine guns
Gonna hunt down all the poachers
Won't you join me for some fun?

HUMBLE

Getting old means getting droopy
Always cold—pants often poopy
Part of life—no need to grumble
It's God's plan to make us humble

POACHERS

The poachers butchered the Rhino's face
so they could get her horn
And then they killed her five year old calf
and left her there to mourn

I saw her face in the paper
and Lord I wanted to cry
The pain of losing her only calf
resonates when you look in her eye

Oh Lord be done with poachers
Do whatever it is it takes
Send them bites from many Cobras
and other venomous snakes

The poacher is the lowest of low
Hunt them wherever they hide
Do the world a favour
It's justified homicide

This garbage—it must be removed
Must be hunted down and killed
Dig a deep and massive grave
Don't stop until it's filled

Coin Toss

In Catholic churches
evil lurches
underneath the loin

You get a good
or evil priest
Same odds to toss a coin

Room for One

Dr. Jeckle doesn't live here
There's no one else inside
There's only room for one in here
and his name's Mr. Hyde

I spend my time inside a rhyme
The rest is all just filler
If I wasn't the poet that I am
I'd surely be a killer

WANNABE

The wannabe musician
thinks he's better than the rest
Think's he has had a higher calling
Thinks he's better than the best

Thinks that everyone's a poser
and that he's the next best thing
He can barely play his instrument
and man can he not sing

He lives inside a dream world
and he's sheltered from the storm
His thought train isn't normal
Pot can rot what is the norm

THINK TANK

Think Tank—what a prank
Preying on the feeble
That one's thinking different thoughts
Give him shock or needle

Keep them muzzled when they're up
Tied down when they're sleeping
Keep the curtains drawn up tight
Want nobody peeping

Keep the voltage high—Lights low
Get their concentration
Get the facts we need to know
then induce vegetation

Keep their hands tied at all times
It keeps them off the ceiling
Once they learn to climb the walls
they regain little feeling

If the feeling starts to grow
It spreads just like a cancer
Just as lethal if you're slow
You might not know the answer

BEGGAR

See the beggar, no disguise
Make no contact with their eyes
Look away, no compromise
Pick up your pace and walk right by

Internally you criticize
That is how you justify
Believe you me you are no prize
One day you may just wear their size

CHAMPION

Saw a man beg for money at the subway station
Had his doggy by his side
That showed me that he had more compassion
than all the ones that passed him by

I look at this man and can't help but think
of what a champion I see
If they were out on the street, forced to beg just to eat
I wonder, where would their pet be

Bucket List

I got it on my bucket list
I want to take a trip
Consume some shrooms
The light show looms
Get swallowed by my fire pit

Water Walker

Jesus walked on water
and he taught me how to swim
He died on cross for all of us
Would you do the same for him

Super Jerk

I just finished my coffee
and I can't drive very far
with this bloody empty coffee cup
sitting in my car

I cannot have it lingering
Awaiting garbage can
The sight of it's appalling
Must come up with other plan

I come up with a solution
as I'm driving into work
I'll just throw it out the window
and become a super—jerk

CECIL THE LION

Cecil the Lion
was the master of two prides
until Walter James Palmer
killed him just to keep his hide

This pathetic little dentist
kills animals for pleasure
Lured Cecil from a National Park
A slaughter made to measure

He shot Cecil with a crossbow
then stalked him for forty hours
Then killed him with a rifle
Psycho's crave this kind of power

And the proof is in the pudding
or in his hand out photograph
Beaming behind the corpse of Cecil
is this smiling psychopath

He killed more than just one lion
He killed the cubs of Cecil's prides
When the male lions come to kill them
they'll have no place they can hide

God please right this awful wrong
And please God—I do insist
Send Walter Palmer what he deserves
A lion who hunts dentists

Paradise Found

I stumbled on my paradise
when I was only nine
And ever since I found that place
I want to make it mine

It's got an old log cabin
and an awesome swimming spot
A memory that's all over me
A memory forever caught

Fear

Imagine the fear
that comes with birth
Being born an animal
down on this earth

The fear of the predators
Of the evil of man
Who will go to the dark-side
to fulfill his own plan

THE STRANGER

The stranger came to town
to check around the place
He looked just like a clown
A textured, painted face

He didn't ask us questions
He knew his way around
He listened to suggestions
but didn't make a sound

He didn't want attention
He only wanted facts
I heard a neighbor mention
what she'd heard through the cracks

He kept to his own mission
He bothered not a soul
He made just one incision
but covered up the hole

He wanted to observe us
To see how we'd react
He wanted to obscure us
To watch us all contract

He left us as he came to us
Just vanished in a crowd
He seemed to pass right through us
Like walking through a cloud

DELAYED JUSTICE

O.J. Simpson robbed some friends
Served ten years—then parole
Maybe now some justice
for Ron and for Nicole

THE ABORTION DISTORTION

Justin Trudeau is very firm
Pro-choice is not a maybe
It must always be a women's right
to terminate her baby

Some woman wait for their last breath
after a life of great distortion
And soon they'll meet the children
they terminated through abortion

WENDEL

They'd come to town and push us down
and rub it in our face
Then Wendel Clark would jump the boards
and put them in their place

Toronto is a hockey town
We love our Maple Leafs
When Wendel Clark got in a scrap
the fight was usually brief

Saturday nights in Kalvington
prepared him for the pros
Great player, but what a fighter
as everybody knows

Dread the Night

I dread the night
when nothing is right
and everything's wrong with the world

I stay out of sight
Not a moth—drawn to light
'cause everything tight comes unfurled

LITTLE DOG WITH NO NAME

Number 541 is a little dog
who will never have a name
He was bred to be a lab dog
A concept cruel and so insane

He's just a number now—he'll receive no love
Alone and locked inside a cage
And sure as there's a god above
God surely is enraged

No debate this is pure evil
and it's time that evil paid
for their sacrilege towards animals
and the horrendous hell they've made

These little dogs—yes they are tortured
with their tests and their restraints
And the world gloats on that Canada
as a nation is a saint

You can tell a lot about a nation
by how it treats its animals
And a nation's heart needs a quick kick start
when they act like cannibals

Twelve thousand dogs a year in Canada
That's exactly what they get
Neglect, restraint, and torture
And never someone's pet

So ashamed to be Canadian
Now that I've been shown the truth
We are indeed an evil nation
Animal testing is the proof

JACINE JADRESKO

Jacine Jadresko makes me ill
The psycho hunter that she is
"The more you hate—the more I kill"
She replied to detractors of her biz

She cannot breathe unless she kills
and she'll kill anything
An elephant—no problem
if she wants some ivory bling!

I pray she dies a horrible death
In the jungle—that should be her fate
Eaten alive by a lion or croc
May a gorilla pick her as a mate!

A Daughters Demise

Where arranged marriage is commonplace
unwed daughters must be willing
or angered fathers and her brothers too
may partake in her killing

And where ever this has happened
the stories ending has begun
when the sins of the daughter's father
become the sins of the father's son

Neil Young

Neil Young is the one
who showed the rest the way
Put conscience into rock'n'roll
and saved the farmers day

AUDIO BRUTE

There's a crying baby on the plane
How we wish this baby was a mute
And everybody secretly prays
for a soother or a parachute

There's a migraine circulating on the plane
There—a crying baby ain't so cute
The shrieks are raining on my brain
Oh this baby is an audio brute

HEARTLESS BASTARDS

They dropped me off on a country road
and then they drove away
Miles away they drove back home
Left me here to find my way

I was their pet and don't quite get
what I've done to lose my home
So I hide and cry—quite afraid to die
in the cold and all alone

The awful plight of many cats and dogs
as their world is torn apart
They're discarded just like garbage
by sick bastards with no heart

Some will starve and die of hunger
Some will freeze out in the cold
All suffer with heart that's broken
The hardest truth if truth be told

Big Tipper

God bless all the big tippers
as I deliver pizza pie
If it wasn't for big tippers
my gas tank would be dry

To hell with the non-tippers
If I couldn't laugh I'd cry
Did my sneeze blow with the breeze
and some how find their pizza pie

DON'T SEPARATE

Our master died
I mourn with my brother
Please don't separate us
from each other

We are two cats
who love each other
Please don't separate us
from one another

We're a dog and a cat
We're like sister and brother
Please don't separate us
from each other

Broken Toes

There is one thing a group home knows
Toddlers can't roam with broken toes
They'll only let them out to play
with broken toes—they cannot stray
Don't break their arm or break their nose
You only have to break their toes
So just ignore their anguished pleas
Must keep them on their hands and knees
'Cause one thing every group home knows
a child can't roam with broken toes

This is the one poem I feel I must explain. I was working with a guy named John once and he told me that while visiting a doctor for some ongoing foot/toe issues the doctor had asked him if he had ever been in the care of the Catholic Children's Aid society. When he replied that he had, the doctor proceeded to tell him that he'd seen a lot of cases of "ex-wards" of the C.C.A.S. with toe issues and was told by some that their toes had been broken when they were young and in "care" to prevent them from wandering.

A FATHER'S DISAPPOINTMENT

His hockey career is over
and it didn't end so well
He's his father's disappointment
Didn't make the N.H.L.

Hold your head up son—it's alright
Sort your thoughts and take a breather
So you didn't make the N.H.L.
Your father didn't either

NINE SHADES OF GREEN

Nine shades of green in my garden
Each one a wonder in itself
Nine shades of green in my garden
None I made by myself

It takes a higher power
to work the wonders of the world
whether lettuce or a flower
or a sunken ocean pearl

Nine shades of green in my garden
A miracle one and all
Nine shades of green in my garden
They'll hang around until the fall

DOCTORS

Doctors are great
I cannot berate
Their work—you gotta like it

God bless the Vet
Best doctors I've met
I swear they must be psychic

MASTERS

Most University grads are bright
Yet some are small disasters
They separate like day and night
as some rise to get their Masters

Brighter Shade of Grey

Nelson Mandela what can you say
He blended black and white
And not an easy task this was
He turned darkness to light

Took black and white then added light
A new colour some would say
He made another colour
A brighter shade of grey

THE SICKNESS

The sickness made them do it
and they do it when they can
It forms a new conduit
that will haunt you as a man

And if you're going through it
do escape it if you can
It's old—as history knew it
but was not part of God's plan

HUMANIMAL

What is a Humanimal
Does anybody know
What I've been told from days of old
They came here long ago

They rode in with the devil
Set up camp and never left
They saw an opportunity
to carry out a theft

They'll steal away your spirit
Suck out your inner soul
They'll tear you down—spin you around
and leave you with a hole

They're quite an ugly creature
I'm talking from within
As some are very beautiful
All wear the human skin

They're liars—they're conniving
and their ego is to blame
They tell the longest stories
but they've got the shortest names

You won't at first take notice
but they've got the longest arms
They'll shake your hand and knife your back
Seduce you with their charms

They dress in different costumes
but the skin they're in's the same
It comes in different colours
Lack of conscience is to blame

Pinocchio

Did he or didn't he
I'm talking 'bout Donald Trump
Did he take the porn star
for a one night hump

Some think yes, some say no
Did he partake in this affair?
This question I can't answer
because I wasn't there

But if I were a gambling man
I bet she told the truth
Trump lies and lies and lies and lies
Within those lies there lies the proof

He brags that he's a genius
but that's just a charade
His lawyer testified under oath
that he was told to hide Trump's grades

It's absurd enough—I've heard enough
It's all one continual spoof
He believes if you lie and lie and lie
The lie becomes the truth

If Donald were a cartoon
he'd be Pinocchio
And one thing is for certain
His nose would grow and grow

Piranha Dorothea Puente

Dorothea Puente was a little old lady
and quite an evil bitch
Killed nine—confirmed, fifteen believed
A serial killer witch

Found seven bodies buried in her yard
Some believed buried alive
The tenants in Dorothea's rooming house
All poisoned—none survived

Killed them, then cashed their pension cheques
Her motive fuelled by greed
A bi-spectacled piranha
and all piranha's feed

MENNONITE DOG

I'm a Mennonite dog
and this is my home
on a Mennonite farm
where I'm all alone

I never get petted
They show no affection
The children ignore me
No love—just rejection

The cold barn in the winter
I freeze all night long
How I long to be loved
How I long to belong

I need a new family
who's able to love
Who follows examples
from God up above

Momar Gadhafi

Gadhafi lost his power
Gadhafi lost his throne
Gadhafi lost his temper
So Gadhafi killed his own

Gadhafi's Karma came round
It came by way of lead
Gadhafi gave out bullets
Took a bullet in the head

A Few Good Friends

A few good friends
is all you need
to stand by you
while others feed

CRIMINALS

The West Detention Centre
was chalk full of retards
I'm not talking bout the inmates
Rather talking 'bout the guards

The large bald bastard threatened me
The threat was not subliminal
These guards conduct—some kind of crime
These guards were the real criminals

Innocent Man

The innocent man
you put in jail
should leave you with no doubt
You now can live a carefree life
but wait 'till he gets out

Life goes on while he's inside
Mind races—blood is boiling
He wears jail garb
and you—pressed pants
The one's you'll soon be soiling

FINAL STRAW

For years and years
they liked to stack
the hay upon
the Camels back

They wait to hear
the mighty crack
The straw that broke
the camels back

Court Order

Court order, Court order
You're a useless piece of paper
He plans his murder/suicide
His last and final caper

Short order—Court order
You're a dangerous piece of paper
He kills then commits suicide
That paper caused this caper

MARY BALE

Let's build a jail
for Mary Bale
and throw away the key

The psychopath
who torments cats
is sick for all to see

Instead of jail
take Mary Bale
for an outing at the zoo

With crowd in rage
throw her in cage
and let the lions chew

It was Mary Bale
locked cat in pale
Pathetic British bitch

She hides her horns
and tail with thorns
This evil wicked witch

BARE MINIMUM

If you go through life
like a closed jack-knife
when you should be like a sword
If you always do bare minimum
that is your reward

HIGH HEELS OR RUNNING SHOES

He's feeling a little straight today
Last night he was quite gay
And who knows who he'll meet tonight
He might go either way

The joy of being bi-sexual
He never has to choose
One night high heels parked under bed
The next it's running shoes

ACCUSATION

First accusation—water's cold
Is there a story to be told
Second accusation—water's warm
There's a calm before the storm

Third accusation—water's hot
You're innocent—or maybe not
Fourth accusation—water boils
Your name and reputation soils

Fifth accusation—making steam
In a nightmare from a dream
Sixth accusation—cannot rest
Take a lie detector test

Did the question send a chill
Honest answer—will you Bill
One liners won't help you now
Your gig is up please take a bow

QUIT YER TWITTER

The kids all drowned and the house burnt down
Gotta blame the babysitter
who was unaware of the smoke filled air
as she thumb-chats via twitter

HUMANIMALS

Humanimals are animals
with many shades of skin
Some eat their greens but in time of need
will often eat your kin

Humanimals hunt the vulnerable
Their favourite choice of prey
Some fill the breeze with their disease
Disease delays decay

Humanimals are cannibals
Will often eat their young
Humanimals have tentacles
and poison drips from tongue

Humanimals are substantial
At work they lurk—some roam
Could be next door—prepare for war
Hang garlic in your home

Blank

Blank verse poets
think they know it
Oh how they like to rant

They try to rhyme
but in short time
they realize they can't

Larry Nassar

Doctor Larry Nassar—what can you say
He turned his patients into prey
In the courtroom they had their day
He's now forever locked away

He lived inside a twisted world
but he abused the bravest girls
They stood up to him and turned the page
He's where he should be—in a cage

LOVELY COTTAGE WITH A CURSE

I was going to rent a lovely cottage
A home right by the lake
I was promised that lovely cottage
but then along came a snake

He took my lovely cottage
He took my lovely home
So I made him a curse of venom and bees
and I sent that curse to roam

He said it wasn't permanent
That he'd only be there a year
A year went by—he didn't fly
Stayed on to drink some beer

In the thirteenth month he guzzled
a beer which held a bee
He died that day—no foul play
Also no sympathy

Was it the curse or a cursed cottage
I can not get that down
because the tenants just before him
were three boys who all drowned

THE CURSE

Mother Nature if you please
With by wind or slight of breeze
Send him venom brought by bees
Knock him to his bloody knees

Warning

It's better not to piss me off
If you piss me off—you do
'Cause I can write a nasty poem
especially for you

And here's an odd twist to it
My poems sometimes come true
It happened to the snake
I'm sure it could happen to you

Chicken or Egg

What came first the chicken or the egg
And if you really care
They synchronize each others lives
It proves that God is there

The answer does not answer
The question realized
Death and Birth come to this earth
but never polarize

SICK LEAVE

Office worker, Office worker
Oh won't you stay at home
You come to work all sickly
That's where your germs will roam

I just may show up at your door
when I am deathly sick
And when my germs come back at you
You'll get yours -you prick!

The Spider

Grim reaper
A creeper of sorts
I'm getting used to it now

Thee cheater
A litre or quart
It's oozing out of us now

Detention
Prevention they say
I'm getting used to the view

Infection
Injection will lay
the creature out for the crew

Survivor
A lifer—no quitter
is training hard for the bout

The spider
It grew down inside her
It grew and ate its way out

Kept spinning
Its webs and was pinning
anyone that came along

Not winning
in end or beginning
Its web just wasn't that strong

COFFEE CASHIER

Where'd they get that cashier
This sight you gotta see
He can't comprehend what's on the screen
His fingers' buzzing round like bee

He's confused and in a panic
Come on, just push a key
Some older guy, he's not a teen
That cashier, that was me

SOMETHING EVIL

Something evil grows
where the soul once had a home
Something evil knows
that one day evil will roam

Something evil planted
in the bastards long before
Ingest and manifest
They are evil to the core

Hatred

Hatred's overrated
Hatred is a chore
My hatred is inflated
and consumes me to my core

Hatred's an affliction
An addiction no one should bare
And now it's my addiction
and with you I'd like to share

Humanimal Zoo

I'm usually right on cue
Sometimes without a clue
But let me warn you now my friend
I can be humanimal too

I leave that up to you
Depends on what you do
When I get torn, I get reborn
Like you—Humanimal too

The amount of Humanimals grew
The others only a few
And now it's insane, the others remain
contained in Humanimal zoo

The ingredients we all knew
Make it hard but soft to chew
Start with the heart—slice it apart
when preparing Humanimal stew

Cauliflower Ears

The professional fighter
He's been fighting now for years
And all he's got to show for it
is Cauliflower ears

He's never won a title
He's spilt blood, sweat, and tears
It's a hard life for a fighter
Not the career of all careers

ONCE A FRIEND

When friends attack
you can never go back
You can never regain that trust

When friends run away
you can never again play
That friendship is a bust

Ridiculous

Johnny got suspended
He got sent home for the day
He wished someone "Merry Christmas"
instead of "Happy holiday"

To be politically correct
you must be so meticulous
How did well wishing get offensive?
It's getting quite ridiculous!

GOD

Have no fear 'cause God is near
Have no lust if God you trust
Have no greed if God you heed
Tell no lies 'cause God has eyes
Worry not—give God that thought

Hidden Message

Find the hidden message
And find the only answer
In the index—of this life
Hatred spreads like cancer

The Clue

Read the first line
And half of the third
Then back to the second

Don't waste time
Do third backward
The second will beckon

Aussie Aboriginals

Aussie Aboriginals
The race whites tore apart
The only race—original
The only race led by the heart

CHRISTINE DANIEL (ANGEL OF DEATH)

The patients lined up one by one
All dying of cancer
All came for cure that was assured
Christine Daniel had the answer

She was a Pentecostal Preacher
and a doctor—yes indeed
But a vile and repugnant creature
chalk full of evil and greed

Claimed she had the cure in a bottle
and was available at a great cost
Five grand a week was her fee—guaranteed
Without it your life would be lost

Many lost their life's savings
No one was cured and all died
Succumbed to the cancer she promised to cure
They died premature 'cause she lied

Christine Daniel made millions
Christine Daniel got rich
She got fourteen years in a prison
She should have got life—evil bitch!

IMPEDIMENT

I have a speech impediment
I pronounce my F's like P's
Some asshole ridiculed me
This asshole liked to tease

He'd tease me at the playground
He'd tease me during school
He'd tease me all around town
This guy's a Puckin' Pool

Not a Word

Don't tell them you're a writer
It's better not to say
When dealing with the terrorists
it could go either way

You better pay attention
and pray the way they pray
Practice means prevention
Delay your execution day

JOAN LAWRENCE

God bless Joan Lawrence
The cat lady of Huntsville
A poet and a gentle soul
Her killer I'd like God to kill

LESSER MAN

The jail guard's leering at me
He proceeds with the strip search
I spread my cheeks, he grins, he peeks
I'm nervous, he does lurch

No entry—strictly exit
Forget about my rear
Nothing's going to enter
Nothing ever goes up here

I offer oral service
He readily agrees
I got a plan—soon lesser man
as I get on my knees

He's ready for his pleasure
but it will never be
My teeth grind hard with no regard
and now he is a she

My Rock

I got to do my writing
'cause my writing is my rock
My rock to knock Goliath out
To break the mental block

Maybe all the readers
make believers of the flock
Swarm all of the leaders
Flock of doves can beat a hawk

Lovely Garden

She glanced upon his little bulge
but what she didn't know
If she should choose to so indulge
How big that bulge would grow

'Cause Jack had him a beanstalk
when he had seeds to sow
And while in her lovely garden
Jack would hoe this lovely ho

Nasty Little Book

If you read this book and hate it
and you hide it on the shelf
Could it be you couldn't take it
when you read about yourself

I just wrote it—you create it
I observe all by myself
If you do choose to berate it
please do keep it to yourself

CANADIAN LABS FROM HELL

The little puppies wag their tails
unaware of what awaits
On there way to a Canadian lab
Neglect and torture is their fate

Puppies, monkeys and little pigs
They all share this brutal end
But Canada's such a great country
That's what we all pretend

I'm sorry, Canada has its evil
Behind locked doors there lies the proof
Through out Canada's darkened labs
animals are tortured and that's the truth

These animals are on an assembly line
and no one heeds their cries
Their life is all torture and terror
by lab technicians—they're brutalized

If the puppies, and monkeys, and piggies could vote
They'd all vote to be euthanized
We allow this brutality to happen
and still claim that we're civilized

CONSCIENCE

Doctor, Doctor
Gimme a pill
to wipe out my conscience
Please go for the kill

This world I can't take it
This world ain't for me
With conscience can't make it
With conscience—can't see

The view—it ain't pretty
The smells even worse
And ain't it a pity
A conscience is curse

A curse in a world
all surrounded in hell
More bad souls than good souls
and you cannot tell

You can't tell the difference
Can't tell them apart
The one's with indifference
from the ones with no heart

Kind soul—please tread softly
Don't awaken the dead
It all could get costly
if they get in your head

A SMALLER WALL

"I'll build a wall" I hear Trump call
He treats people like they're cargo
If he really wants to build a wall
Build a wall around Mar-a-Lago

China Zoo

The little dog shivers
The little dog shakes
He knows he's the next meal
of that big bad snake

The dog's in the snake's pen
The people they can't wait
To see this terrified dog
get eaten by the snake

The giant snake strikes
The people all cheer
The little dog yelps
He'll get no help here

The dog cries and yes
The people they all laugh
The expected response
of a true psychopath

Beijing Take Out

They line up all the little dogs
and beat them all alive
They claim that they taste better
when they die terrified

The logic is retarded
The mood malevolent
Of this evil behaviour
You must be evil to invent

Istanbul

God bless the people of Istanbul
With stray cats they are so kind
In Istanbul they bathe in light
and other cities are so blind

Asian Cats

The Asian cats are terrified
Locked in a cage and petrified
Try to avoid the iron tongs
around their neck and then they're fried

EVERYTHING THEY DO

I don't hate the Chinese people
No, no, no, no, nooo
But some people back in China
I hate everything they do

They terrorize, then kill and eat
puppy dogs—who knew
Other dogs they feed the snake
at their God-damned zoo

An equal evil fate for cats
in this man made-hell
And anywhere where evil's made
is where the evil dwells

Free Sample

God gave humans animals
and sent them from above
To give us a free sample
of his unconditional love

EUTHANASIA PLEASE

Euthanized at one or two
And that is this dogs blessing
A year or two of torture
Burned and blistered—there's no dressing

She's a lab dog and no different
than the pooch you have at home
Restrained and force fed toxins
She gets no love and gets no bone

Your make-ups safe because of her
and God never gave that rite
To torture loving creatures
and hide it out of site

It's reality in Canada
It's a doggie holocaust
And for us to all allow it
proves our empathy is lost

It's reality in the western world
No one seems to give a crap
We collectively become Hitler
No dog deserves this human trap

Up in good ol' Canada
Twelve thousand dogs a year share this fate
Also five-thousand monkeys
Don't tell me Canada's great

Shameful

You take a dog that's full of love
Teach it to harm on cue
What is now wrong with this dog
is what is wrong with you

To take its love and create hate
is evil that you grew
And you're to blame, should be ashamed
The shame is all on you

THE CIRCLE SPINS

Eternal life
or final death
You breathe in air
then lose your breath

You spread the hate
with brand new lungs
Bad Karma waits
for poison tongues

Equations play
their part in life
Karma will cut
down those with knife

You'll reap the harvest
you have sown
Like boomerang
those stones you've thrown

The moon reflects
the sun at night
The sun deflects
the hate with light

The world spins all
of us around
while gravity
just wears us down

Your flesh exists
to house your soul
Your hatred's nothing
but a mole

The mole does grow
The flesh decays
and makes a nightmare
of your days

It consumes you
It eats away
Then spits you out
and finds new prey

The circle spins
but goes nowhere
and no one wins
No prize to share

CHOCOLATES FOR MOM

They gobble chocolates they didn't earn
as they sit on their fat fannies
A mother's day gift from their children
that should have gone to their nannies

My mother eats her chocolates
given to her by her son
And she deserves a billion boxes
'cause she earned every one

Family Member from Hell

I have a family member
who's tongue is like a dart
And when she opens up her mouth
out comes a verbal fart

She farts and farts and farts and farts
She has a smelly mouth
She farts from northern hemispheres
Her brain—it migrates south

She's in everybody's business
Everywhere she shouldn't be
She's always got the answer
Missed the question completely

Remembrance Day

On Remembrance day we honour those
who lost or risked their lives
If we could go back and take their place
we'd all be terrified

DIRK THE JERK

The devil's taken human form
in Ahlen, Germany
Dirk Schlebes' heart is concrete
and it's as cold as cold can be

Dirk the jerk's the treasurer
in Ahlen, Germany
And if you can't pay your taxes
your dog becomes the fee

Edda was a sweet dog
who loved her family
But Dirk Schlebes wanted money
so poor Edda became history

The bastard sold Edda Online
in lieu of taxes owing
Now Edda's never coming home
since Schlebes decided she was going

Come try and take my dog away
for taxes in arrear
'Cause if you do you asshole
I guarantee you'll disappear

A Poet's Lament

To understand a poet's lament
It's like the need to pee while in a warm tent
We lie in bed all wrapped up warm
A line appears and then words swarm
A poem is forming in our head
and to save this poem we must leave our bed
Climb out of the warmth—we seek paper and ink
We must lasso that poem—save it from the brink
We can't ignore this urge—we must soldier on
If we fall asleep that poem is long gone

Botswana's Shame

You can fly down to Botswana
and pay to kill an Elephant
You deserve to get Ebola
if you go with that intent

Zimbabwe is no better
It's just a higher price you'll pay
Both have governments—pure evil
If you're a tourist—stay away!

SHRINKAGE

She walked in the wrong change room
and caught an eyeful when she did
Jimmies dong was well exposed
If he had time he would have hid

Jimmy was an exhibitionist
but this scene just wasn't cool
For Jimmy had just gotten out of
a fairly chilly swimming pool

The chilly water took its toll
and Jimmy's pecker paid the price
His bountiful jumbo sausage
had shrunken to a piece of rice

The girl assumed that was his normal size
but what she didn't know
The penis is a strange fellow
The way they shrink and grow

The penis is a chameleon
And yes there's no debate
After swimming it's three inches long
Before sex it grows to eight

The plight of the poor penis
She doesn't realize
To be effective in between us
it must grow to its full size

When you're young they stand to attention
When you're old they limp around
Thank God for magic little blue pills
Now older guys can stand their ground

The moral to this story
Don't be a bloody fool
When you take her on your first date
don't take her to a swimming pool

KITCHEN HELPER

I'm working at the restaurant
and nothings going right
If left to my devises
No one eats tonight

At least not what they ordered
I might just get it wrong
You ordered Calamari
I gave you four Won Ton

You want a Caesar salad
Well Caesar—he left town
I'll get it right around midnight
Now eat your spinach and calm down

You want a starter salad
Well you just might have to wait
My biggest struggle here by far
Is figuring what goes on what plate

The orders they're all clustered
and coming at warp speed
And hell I'm getting flustered
Can't seem to get out of the weeds

James Forcillo

Toronto cop James Forcillo
dropped a boy to the floor
Dropped him with three bullets
then shot him six times more

This happened on a vacant streetcar
The boy had a pocket knife
Forcillo served two years in prison
He should have gotten life

Free Will

Free will causes pollution
and free will causes war
Free will is no solution
but it's free so we want more

Free will is what we wanted
Free will is what we got
Free will has left us haunted
as free will can make you rot

Free will can cause addiction
Free will won't set us free
Free will is an affliction
Sends us drifting in a sea

Free will will not enlighten
Free will will shed no light
Free will may blind in time
and send us scurrying in the night

Free will comes to an end
when we return after we die
That's when the truth arrives
and then no one can live a lie

Unconditional Love

You're looking for unconditional love
You're looking round for God
If you want unconditional love on earth
get yourself a cat or dog

Both are gifts that God has given us
so you better treat them well
And to those who choose to abuse them
God reserves a special hell

MONSTER KIM JONG UN

The devil sent another monster
since Hitler left the room
And this one's just as evil
His name is Kim Jong Un

His people applaud and cheer him
In truth they live a lie
This idiot thinks they love him
Truth be told they're terrified

They know the ramifications
if they don't cheer and applaud
If they show no love for this monster
they'll face his firing squad

May Karma come at God speed
for this reptile of a man
Killed in some freak accident
I'm sure God's got a plan

Cigarettes

Cigarettes, Cigarettes
will bring you nothing but regrets
The damage done you can't forget
Throw away those bloody cigarettes

EVIL KIM JONG UN

No one will envy Kim Jong Un
when this sick bastard dies
Lives a life he feels owes no reproach
He's in for some surprise

He thinks he gets a pass from God
for all the evil he's created
And this sick bastards pure evil
This need not be debated

His people are fed a diet of dog
North Korean dogs are eaten
And Kim Jong Un is the bastard who states
that dogs taste better if beaten

Taste better if they're beaten to death?
If they die terrified?
Only a heartless monster
could believe that thought is justified

I got a message for Mr. Kim Jong Un
In death you will discover
Karma that's owed for the seeds that you've sowed
will be dealt out by God—a dog lover!

Little Black Cat

Sitting at the pound getting old and fat
Few will take home a little black cat
If they euthanize they're the first to go
They're on death row—they don't even know
They give you so much love—I'll attest to that
Please take home that little black cat

Diss-ease

The reason meat will kill you
It's the diss—ease at the slaughter
The meat holds all bad vibes
Could make a ripple in the water

Stressed pigs and cows and anguished sows
The diss—ease must return
Comes back at humans as disease
and it's anybody's turn

A quick suggestion—don't ask the question
now that you know the answer
We cause diss—ease, then get disease
and it often comes back as cancer

VIRUS

In China they beat stray dogs to death
The spread of virus—they think they prevent
The question they need to ponder
Is their cruelty to dogs why the virus was sent?

INFERNO

If you believe in God
Start acting like you do
If you hurt and kill God's creatures
You'll meet a God you never knew

Good luck in the eternal
They'll be no sympathy
You'll be stuck in the inferno
We all choose our destiny

"The only thing necessary for the triumph of evil is for good men to do nothing" ~ Edmund Burke

"You are a child of God. Your playing small doesn't serve the world. There's nothing enlightened about shrinking so that other people won't feel insecure around you." ~From Nelson Mandela's Inaugural Speech 1994